MONSTERS in MYTH

THE CYCLOPES

MONSTERS in MYTH

Titles in the Series

MONSTERS in MYTH

THE CYCLOPES

RUSSELL ROBERTS

Mitchell Lane
PUBLISHERS

P.O. BOX 196
HOCKESSIN, DELAWARE 19707
VISIT US ON THE WEB: WWW.MITCHELLLANE.COM
COMMENTS? EMAIL US: MITCHELLLANE@MITCHELLLANE.COM

Printing   1   2   3   4   5   6   7   8   9

Library of Congress Cataloging-in-Publication Data
Roberts, Russell, 1953–
   The cyclopes / by Russell Roberts.
       p. cm. — (Monsters in myth)
   Includes bibliographical references and index.
   ISBN 978-1-58415-926-1 (library bound)
   1. Cyclopes (Greek mythology)—Juvenile literature. I. Title.
   BL820.C83R63 2011
   398.20938'01—dc22
                                                                      2010006556

ABOUT THE AUTHOR: Russell Roberts has written and published nearly 40 books for adults and children on a variety of subjects, including baseball, memory power, business, New Jersey history, and travel. He has written numerous books for Mitchell Lane Publishers, including *Nathaniel Hawthorne, Holidays and Celebrations in Colonial America, What's So Great About Daniel Boone, Poseidon, The Life and Times of Nostradamus*, and *The Minotaur.* He lives in Bordentown, New Jersey, with his family and a fat, fuzzy, and crafty calico cat named Rusti.

AUTHOR'S NOTE: Portions of this story have been retold using dialogue as an aid to readability. The dialogue is based on the author's extensive research and approximates what might have occurred at the time.

PUBLISHER'S NOTE: This story is based on the author's extensive research, which he believes to be accurate. Documentation of such research is contained on page 46.

The internet sites referenced herein were active as of the publication date. Due to the fleeting nature of some web sites, we cannot guarantee they will all be active when you are reading this book.

To reflect current usage, we have chosen to use the secular era designations BCE ("before the common era") and CE ("of the common era") instead of the traditional designations BC ("before Christ") and AD (*anno Domini,* "in the year of the Lord").

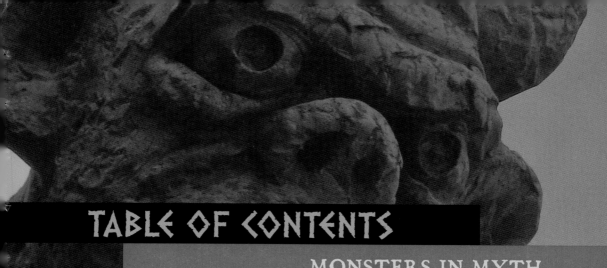

TABLE OF CONTENTS

MONSTERS IN MYTH

THE CYCLOPES

A modern Cyclops sand sculpture. The appearance of the Cyclops is limited only by one's imagination—the only requirement is that he have just one eye.

CYCLOPES

CHAPTER 1

Trapped!

Odysseus (oh-DIH-see-us) and his men were tired. The Greek general (known to the Romans as Ulysses) and his men had been away from their homes for ten arduous years. They had been fighting against a faraway city called Troy (located in modern-day Turkey). The Trojans were fierce warriors. They had been holed up safely inside their walled city, and it had been nearly impossible for the Greeks to defeat them. Many Greeks grew tired and frustrated. They yearned to see their homes and families again.

Finally, when all seemed lost, Odysseus came up with the idea of building a giant, hollow wooden horse, hiding Greek soldiers inside it, and then pretending that the rest of the Greeks had sailed away. When the Trojans saw the wooden horse sitting on the beach all by itself, with no enemy soldiers in sight, they assumed that the Greeks had finally given up and gone home. Figuring the horse was a gift, they brought it inside the city while they decided what to do with it.

That night, in honor of their victory, the Trojans celebrated. But then, while Troy slept, the Greeks inside the horse snuck out, killed the guards, and opened the gates, allowing the rest of the Greek soldiers—who had come back—into the city. The Greeks destroyed Troy, thus winning the war.

Now Odysseus and his men were finally sailing home. What they did not know was that they had a long and perilous journey ahead of them, and that only Odysseus would make it home. This story is told in *The Odyssey*—an epic poem by Homer.

Once Odysseus and his men had left Troy and set sail for home, storms churned up the ocean and ill winds blew their ship far off course. Waves crashed against the boat, the wind howled, rain pelted down on them, and the ship lurched from side to side, tossed like a feather on a breeze. The Greeks had to use all their sailing skills to keep their ship from being destroyed.

At last the weather calmed down, and the ship reached an island. It had mountains that were so high their tops were hidden by clouds. Waves from the sea roared and crashed against rocky cliffs. It did not seem to be a place that welcomed visitors, but the Greeks were tired. They needed food, water, and rest. Despite the island's inhospitable appearance, they decided to go ashore.

Once the ship was anchored, Odysseus selected twelve of his men to scout the island with him for food and water. They brought some wine, which they hoped to trade for food. After searching, the Greeks found a large cave in one of the mountains. Inside the cave were great baskets filled with fruit, cheese, and vegetables. The Greeks decided to wait in the apparent home for the owner to return, and then ask him to share some of his food with them. In ancient Greece, the rules of hospitality, called *xenia,* dictated that strangers be treated with kindness, and that strangers respect their hosts. Zeus was the god of supplicants—those who have a request—so to break the rules of *xenia* was to anger the ruler of the gods.

The longer they waited, the more Odysseus's heart filled with dread. Next to the cave's opening was a giant boulder that was obviously being used as a door. What type of man could push a rock that size? Even if Odysseus and all of his men tried, they wouldn't be able to budge it.

Another thing that worried Odysseus was the size of the baskets that held the food. They were enormous! How big was the man who needed baskets of food that size?

As the sun began to set, Odysseus found the terrible answer to his questions. First a herd of sheep came spilling into the cave. Then, behind them, a giant man crawled inside. He was the largest and tallest man any of the Greeks had ever seen, with shaggy hair and a scraggly beard. However, his immensity wasn't the most amazing thing about him.

He had but one eye . . . and it was in the middle of his forehead! He was a Cyclops (SY-klops).

After the Cyclops was inside, he rolled the giant boulder across the opening, closing the cave. Odysseus and his men were trapped with this monstrous creature! Terrified by his great size and strange appearance, they shrank back against a wall of the cave.

Suddenly the giant spied the Greeks. "Who are you who enter unbidden [uninvited] the house of Polyphemus [pahl-ee-FEE-mus]?" he roared. "Traders or thieving pirates?"[1]

Bravely Odysseus stepped forward. "Shipwrecked warriors from Troy are we, and your supplicants, under the protection of Zeus, the supplicants' god."[2]

Odysseus was hoping that the mention of Zeus, king of the gods and of the sky, would make the giant treat them kindly. To his dismay, Polyphemus laughed contemptuously and said that he didn't care about Zeus. He was bigger than any god, he continued, and didn't fear any of them.

Then, as if to make his point, the Cyclops stretched out his great arm and grabbed two of Odysseus's men. The men screamed as Polyphemus raised them high in the air. As the rest of the horrified Greeks watched, the giant ate the two men. He then washed down his terrible meal with some sheep's milk, rolled over, and went to sleep.

Too scared to sleep, the Greeks listened to Polyphemus snore throughout the night. Odysseus knew that the monster would eventually eat all of them. He had to think of a plan to escape!

But how? The boulder blocked the cave's entrance. They could not move it. If they were to kill Polyphemus as he slept, they would die inside the cave. If they did not kill the Cyclops, however, then they would surely die themselves.

Once Polyphemus had trapped Odysseus and his sailors inside his great cave, the Greeks were at the giant's mercy. The creature devoured some of the helpless humans.

When morning came, Polyphemus awoke and ate two more of the Greeks. Then he moved the boulder so that the sheep could go outside to graze. After he crawled out of the cave, the giant reached over and pushed the rock back in front of the opening.

The Greeks were trapped. Were they doomed to wait there to be eaten two by two by this hideous giant? What could they do?

The Trojan War

The Trojan War, thought to have occurred from 1194 to 1184 BCE is one of the most important events of the ancient world. It is a key part of Greek mythology and was written about by many cultures. Homer's epic work *The Iliad* is about the last few weeks of the ten-year war. While *The Odyssey* is about the ten years after the war, it also contains news of it.

According to Greek myth, the war had its roots in a quarrel among the gods. Eris (EE-ris), the goddess of discord, gave a golden apple that she labeled "for the fairest" to the goddesses Athena (uh-THEE-nuh), Hera (HAYR-uh), and Aphrodite (af-roh-DY-tee). However, since Eris never identified which particular goddess was "the fairest," the three couldn't agree on who should have the apple.

To settle the argument, Zeus (ZOOS) sent the three goddesses to Paris, the son of King Priam (PRY-am) of Troy, and had him choose "the fairest." Paris picked Aphrodite, infuriating the other two. In return, Aphrodite made Helen, the most beautiful woman in the world, fall in love with Paris. However, Helen was already married to Menelaus (men-uh-LAY-uhs), king of Sparta. Paris fled with Helen to Troy, and Menelaus's brother King Agamemnon (ag-uh-MEM-non) of Mycenae led an army of Greek soldiers against Troy to avenge the insult.

The war lasted ten years. During most of the time the Greeks besieged Troy, which was a walled city, but could never figure out how to get inside. Finally, Odysseus (perhaps with the help of Athena) devised the idea of building a hollow wooden horse and hiding soldiers inside it. The Trojans brought the horse into the city, and Troy was destroyed.

Mosaic of Uranus and Gaia, Munich, Germany. Every culture has a creation story, and the Greeks were no different. Their story begins with Chaos and concludes with Zeus and his fellow Olympians becoming the rulers of the universe.

CYCLOPES

CHAPTER 2

The Birth—and Death— of the Cyclopes

In Greek mythology, there are two generations of Cyclopes (sy-kloh-PEEZ; the plural of *Cyclops*). The first were involved in the birth of the world. The second were descended from Poseidon (puh-SY-dun), god of the sea. It was this second group of creatures—and specifically Polyphemus—with whom Odysseus ran into trouble. However, the first generation of Cyclopes were not harmful. They liked and respected the gods (as compared to Polyphemus's contempt for Zeus), and they were helpful.

The Greeks used myths to explain things that they did not understand. Just as all cultures have done since humanity first appeared on earth, the Greeks wondered how the world developed and how people came to live in it. It was only natural for them to devise myths about the beginning of the world. The first generation of Cyclopes played a critical role in this story.

In the very beginning, before anything, they believed, there was just emptiness. There was nothing except a big, black void that went on forever and ever. The Greeks called this nothingness Chaos.[1] Then, from out of Chaos, the earth appeared. The earth was called Gaia, or Gaea (JEE-uh, or GY-uh). The earth is the exact opposite of Chaos. The earth is solid and firm. All things come from Gaia—forests, mountains, oceans, and life.

Gaia gave birth to Uranus (YUR-uh-nus), the Sky; and Pontus, the waters in the sea. Gaia and Uranus then had children known as the Titans.

The next group of children born to Gaia and Uranus were not normal children—they were monsters. As Greek mythology expert Edith Hamilton explains: "Just as we believe that the earth was once inhabited by strange gigantic creatures, so did the Greeks. They did not, however, think of them as huge lizards and mammoths, but as somewhat like men and yet unhuman."[2]

The first set of enormous children was the three Cyclopes, named Brontes (BRAHN-teez), meaning thunder; Steropes (STAYR-oh-peez), meaning lightning; and Arges (AR-geez), meaning brightness. As Hamilton explains, they were called Cyclopes—Wheel-eyed— because "each had only one enormous eye, as round and as big as a wheel, in the middle of the forehead."[3] They were giant beings, as big as mountains.

Another group of children was even more hideous-looking than the Cyclopes. They were the Hecatonchires (heh-kuh-TONG-kuh-reez)—the Hundred-Handed Creatures. They were also exceptionally large, and each had 50 heads and 100 arms.

Unfortunately, Uranus was an uncaring father. He did not like any of his children, so he kept them from leaving Gaia. This did not make her happy, and she groaned from the discomfort of holding them all.

Besides feeling uncomfortable, Gaia also was angry with Uranus for treating their children so badly. She sought help to defeat Uranus. She begged the Titans to confront their father, but they were all afraid to oppose someone as powerful as Uranus. Everyone refused— except the Titan Kronos (KROH-nus). He decided that he would fight his father. Gaia helped him by making a weapon from special material inside the earth. The weapon was a sickle, and with it Kronos could now confront his father. Kronos did indeed fight Uranus using the sickle and won. The victory made Kronos king of the universe. Rhea (REE-uh), another Titan, became his wife.

Kronos was no better a ruler or father than Uranus had been. Suspicious of everyone who was powerful and could do him harm, he imprisoned the three Cyclopes and the Hecatonchires in Tartarus (TAR-tuh-rus). This was the deepest, darkest region of the Underworld—a gloomy pit surrounded by a wall of bronze. There was no escape from Tartarus.

Gaia fed the paranoia of Kronos by warning him that a child of his would grow stronger than he and beat him, just as he had beaten Uranus. To make sure that he would not be overthrown, Kronos swallowed every child of his that Rhea bore. He knew that the children could do no harm to him if they were safely inside his stomach.

Of course, Rhea was as unhappy about this as Gaia was with Uranus's actions. So, just like Gaia did, Rhea decided to fight her husband. The next time Rhea was about to have a baby, she slipped away from Kronos to the island of Crete to deliver the child. She had the baby and entrusted it to some naiads (NAY-adz), nymphs who inhabited non-ocean waters, such as rivers and streams. The naiads took the baby to a deep cave, where they could raise him away from Kronos's prying eyes. Later, when the baby—who was called Zeus— got older and cried loudly, Rhea put some male spirits at the front of the cave and had them do war dances and sing loud songs. The sound covered the baby's cries.

To complete her deception, when he demanded to see the baby, Rhea brought Kronos a rock wrapped in a blanket. "Be careful . . . he's tiny,"[4] she said when she gave him the rock. Kronos immediately swallowed it, little suspecting that he had been tricked.

Meanwhile, on Crete, Zeus grew up. He was young and strong. He decided to make Kronos pay for what he had tried to do to him and what he had done to his brothers and sisters. However, he realized that he needed others to help him defeat Kronos. He (or Rhea) gave Kronos a vile drink that made him vomit up all of her other children. These became the other Olympic gods, plus Hades (HAY-deez) and Poseidon.

Now that he had allies, Zeus needed weapons, and for these he turned to the Cyclopes. He freed them and the Hecatonchires from

To avoid having Kronos swallow all of her children, Rhea gave him a rock wrapped inside a blanket instead of the baby Zeus.

Tartarus. In gratitude, the Cyclopes provided Zeus with the mightiest weapon in the universe—the thunderbolt.

Here again Gaia took a hand. Just as she had provided Kronos with the sickle he needed to defeat Uranus, so too did she help the Cyclopes to manufacture the thunderbolt, providing them with the material they needed.[5] In Zeus's hands the thunderbolt was the ultimate weapon, and just the thing he needed to fight Kronos.

However, the Cyclopes did not stop there. They were master metal-forgers, and they created other weapons. For Zeus's brother Poseidon they created a mighty trident. Hades received a cap of darkness.

Now that Zeus and his brothers and sisters were armed, they waged war against Kronos and the other Titans. This ten-year battle was called the Titanomachy. Finally, after the fighting nearly destroyed the universe, Zeus and his fellows were victorious.

Seventeenth-century Dutch artist Joachim Wtewael depicts the battle between Zeus and his allies against the Titans for control of the universe.

Zeus bound the Titans in chains and hurled them into Tartarus. For the Titan Atlas, however, he had a special punishment. He decreed that he must carry the world on his shoulders forever.

Zeus was very grateful for the help the Cyclopes gave him. As a reward, he let the three Cyclopes live in the universe. They became the master metalworkers of the gods, much like Hephaestus, god of metalworking. Sometimes we find them laboring in Hephaestus's forge, helping him. They are also master builders, and it is they who are given credit for building the walls of Mycenae.

Unfortunately, these three Cyclopes were to come to grief at the hands of another god—Apollo (uh-PAH-loh), the god of light. Apollo could be very hotheaded. This was certainly true when he grew angry with Coronis, a mortal woman he loved. She was pregnant with his child, but then she foolishly fell in love with a mortal man. Apollo found out about this from the crow, a bird which at that time was entirely white.

Furious, Apollo sent his sister Artemis to earth. She killed Coronis and placed her body to burn on a funeral pyre. (Another version says that Apollo himself did the killing.) Once Coronis was dead, Apollo felt terrible, but the deed had already been done. Although Apollo was also the god of healing, even he could not bring the dead back to life.

(Later, Apollo exacted revenge on the crow whose gossip had gotten him into such a rage. In one version, he cursed the bird, turning its feathers black. In another version, the smoke from the burning funeral pyre permanently stained the crow's feathers black.)

Although Apollo could do nothing for Coronis, he could, and did, save his unborn son from the flames. Apollo brought the infant to a centaur named Chiron (KY-ron). Most centaurs were wild and lawless, but Chiron was wise and good. He agreed to raise the child, who was called Asclepius (as-KLEE-pee-us). Because Apollo was the god of healing, Chiron taught the boy the art of medicine and healing.

Apollo (left) visits the god of the forge in *The Forge of the Vulcan* (Hephaestus), Velázquez, 1630. The three Cyclopes are shown as master workers at the forge. They often assisted Hephaestus.

Asclepius became a great physician, helping and healing the sick. His symbol was a physician's staff with a snake curled around it. (A similar symbol is still used to represent the medical profession.) According to some, Asclepius also learned other things, such as incantations and the use of potions. Some say that Athena gave him a potion made from the blood of the Gorgon. If taken from the right side of the Gorgon, the blood could do amazing things, such as bring people back from the dead. However, if taken from the left, the blood was a deadly poison.

Thus Asclepius had the uncanny ability to return life to the dead. There are several stories of his using that ability—he accepted money from people to bring them back, and one time the goddess Artemis begged him to return life to Hippolytus (hih-PAH-luh-tus), son of Theseus (THEE-see-uhs).[6] Either way, Asclepius now had knowledge that no human should have, and he was using it to upset the natural order of things by interfering with life and death.

When Zeus saw what Asclepius was doing, he decided to restore the natural order. From Mount Olympus, he sent a mighty thunderbolt to earth and killed Asclepius.

When Apollo heard that Zeus had killed his son, he was furious. There was nothing he could do to Zeus, because he was all-powerful. He could, however, take revenge on those who had made the thunderbolt that Zeus had used—the three Cyclopes, Brontes, Steropes, and Arges.

Apollo sought out the three Cyclopes and killed them with his arrows. Their spirits are said to live in Mount Etna, an active volcano that smokes and rumbles because of the Cyclopes' metalworking.

When Zeus heard of their deaths, he was furious. He thought about banishing Apollo to Tartarus, but ultimately he decided to make Apollo serve a human being for one year—a very humiliating punishment for a god.

Asclepius

PLEASE DO NOT TOUCH

F.Y.I.

FOR YOUR INFORMATION

Centaurs

The Battle of Centaurs and Lapiths at Hippodamia's Wedding, Karel Dujardin, 1667

In Greek mythology, centaurs—creatures with the lower body of a horse, but the head and upper body of a human—are usually depicted as wild, savage creatures. (An exception is the centaur Chiron, who was kind and wise, and who raised Asclepius.) They lived by following their own laws and rules, and usually when they mingled with humans, they caused trouble. The primary example of this is perhaps the most well-known centaur story of all: the wedding of Hippodamia (hih-poh-DAY-mee-uh).

According to the tale, Hippodamia was going to marry Pirithous, who was related to the centaurs. As relatives, the centaurs attended the wedding.

Once there, however, the centaurs displayed the kind of unruly behavior that had given them a bad name. They drank heavily, and then tried to carry off Hippodamia and the rest of the women. Fortunately, the great hero Theseus was a wedding guest. He, Pirithous, and others managed to drive the centaurs away and rescue the women. It is believed that this story reflects the constant conflict in human society between its good and its lower elements.

In real-life, the model for the centaur may have simply been the first time an ancient culture experienced the sight of people on horseback. They thought that they were seeing people who were actually half human and half animal. This theory is given more weight by the fact that thousands of years later, when the Aztecs first encountered Spaniards riding horses, they reportedly felt that they were seeing creatures that were half human and half animal.

Like the Cyclopes, centaurs have remained popular right up to the present day. Authors C.S. Lewis and J.K. Rowling have featured centaurs in their popular book series *The Chronicles of Narnia* and *Harry Potter,* respectively. Chiron is a main character in Rick Riordan's series *Percy Jackson and the Olympians.*

To escape from the cave of the Cyclops, Odysseus devised a plan. He continually poured wine for Polyphemus to drink, hoping to get him intoxicated.

CYCLOPES

CHAPTER 3

In the Cave of the Beast

As the day wore on near the Cyclops's lair, Polyphemus sat peacefully watching his sheep graze. The bright sun beat down on the land with pleasant warmth.

But in the dark cave that served as the giant's home, there was no sunlight or heat that day. There was only darkness and the foul smell of decaying flesh from the few bones of Odysseus's men that the monster had spit out. The Greek sailors who were left alive were fearful. Was this to be their fate—waiting to be devoured by this horrible creature? They implored Odysseus to think of some way to save them.

Fortunately, Odysseus was already plotting. He ordered his men to pick up a long piece of wood that he had seen lying on the floor of the cave. The Greeks spent the day cutting and trimming the end of the wood until it was as sharp as a spear. Then they hardened the tip in the fire until it was like a diamond. When they were finished, the Greeks hid the log in the shadows and waited for Polyphemus to come back.

Soon the giant returned, and after bringing all his sheep into the cave and replacing the rock in front of the hole, the Cyclops ate two more sailors. After this terrible dinner was complete, Odysseus stepped forward. He still had the wine from the ship, and he offered the Cyclops a cup of it as a gift. Polyphemus gulped the wine down, wiped the back of his hand across his mouth, and demanded more. Odysseus obligingly filled the cup again. Polyphemus tossed this down too, then asked Odysseus his name.

"My friends and relations call me Outis,"[1] Odysseus said. (In Greek, *outis* means "nobody.")[2]

"Outis—Nobody!" bellowed the Cyclops. "Well, since you're Nobody, I'll give you a gift too—I'll eat you last!"[3] Drunk on the wine, and satisfied from his grisly dinner, Polyphemus rolled over on his side and fell asleep.

This was the Greeks' chance—probably their only chance. Odysseus and his men took the sharpened stick out of hiding and heated the point in the fire. Then they plunged the stick into the Cyclops's eye as he lay sleeping.

Polyphemus awoke with a roar. He thrashed around, trying to find the Greeks, but he was now blind, and the humans were able to elude him easily.

Polyphemus's cries alerted the other Cyclopes on the island. They called to him, asking what was wrong.

"Ah, it's terrible, he's killing me!"[4] Polyphemus howled from inside his cave.

The other Cyclopes anxiously asked him who was killing him.

"Nobody!"[5] responded Polyphemus.

When the other Cyclopes heard that "nobody" was hurting Polyphemus, they thought he might just be having a bad dream. They left him alone.

The Greeks were almost out of danger. However, they still had to get out of the cave. In the morning, the blinded Cyclops rolled the rock away from the cave's entrance. He felt the back of the sheep as they went out, hoping to catch the Greeks riding on top of the animals. But Odysseus had tricked Polyphemus again. He had his men tie together three of the sheep with strips of bark. Then, as the sheep left the cave, the men held on *underneath* the animals instead of on top. In this way the Greeks were able to escape from the cave.

Once they were safely aboard their ship, the Greeks quickly set sail to get away from the island of the Cyclopes. However, Odysseus, bitter over the way Polyphemus had treated his men, could not resist a taunting cry from his ship to the giant still on shore: "So, Cyclops, you were not quite strong enough to eat all of the puny

Polyphemus roars as Odysseus flies toward him in this fanciful version of how the Greek warrior blinded the giant.

Odysseus in the Cave of Polyphemus, by Jakob Jordaens, before 1650. Blinding Polyphemus was only half of Odysseus' escape plan. The second part was being able to sneak out of the creature's cave by hiding underneath sheep.

men? You are rightly punished for what you did to those who were guests in your house."[6]

When Polyphemus heard Odysseus laughing at him, he tore off a piece of a nearby cliff and threw it in the direction of the sound. It landed with a tremendous splash very near the ship.

Still, Odysseus was not satisfied. Again he yelled: "Cyclops, Odysseus, wrecker of cities, put out your eye, and do you so tell anyone who asks."[7]

Ulysses Defying the Cyclops, Louis Frédéric Schützenberger. After successfully escaping from the cave of the Cyclops, Odysseus could not resist taunting Polyphemus as his ship quickly sailed away. This bit of vanity would come back to haunt the hero.

By this time the ship was too far away for Polyphemus to reach it, but Odysseus had made a serious error by telling the Cyclops his name. Now the creature could curse the Greeks—which he did. He asked his father Poseidon, the god of the sea, for revenge on Odysseus and his men. He asked that Odysseus not return home to Ithaca without suffering countless disasters—his companions dying, his ship capsizing, himself a castaway. Finally, he asked that if and when Odysseus did return home, that he would be seen as a stranger—not a conquering hero.

Poseidon heard his son's words and obliged. The curse of Polyphemus triggered all the years of wandering and all the trials that Odysseus endured before finally arriving home.

Polyphemus appealed to his father, the god Poseidon, to bring misery down upon the Greeks.

What happened to Polyphemus and what ultimately happened to Odysseus are very similar. By putting out the Cyclops's eye, Odysseus condemned him to a life of wandering aimlessly down pathways that would be forever dark and mysterious. By cursing Odysseus, Polyphemus did the same thing—cursing him to wander about unknowingly.

Polyphemus might have avoided this entire incident if only he had listened to a warning by the prophet Telemus (TEH-luh-mus). While he was visiting the island, Telemus warned Polyphemus that one day in the future, a great hero would come and put out the giant's eye.

Maybe if Polyphemus had not been distracted, he would have listened to Telemus. At the time, the Cyclops had little interest in dire warnings. All he could think about was a beautiful sea nymph named Galatea (gah-luh-TEE-uh).

The Odyssey

The Odyssey is one of the major works of literature of the ancient world. It is partly a sequel to *The Iliad*. Both works are epic poems likely meant to be sung. Both are credited to Homer, although the identity of Homer is a subject of debate. Scholars believe the poems were written at the end of the eighth century BCE in Ionia, which is in modern-day Turkey.

The Odyssey begins ten years after the fall of Troy, and Odysseus has still not returned to his kingdom in Ithaca, or to his wife Penelope (peh-NEL-oh-pee) or son Telemachus (tuh-LEM-uh-kus). Assuming that Odysseus is dead, a large mob of suitors has descended upon his palace, trying to court Penelope. However, Penelope has remained faithful to Odysseus throughout all these years, and she has been holding the suitors off. But time is running out.

Odysseus, meanwhile, is very much alive. Without a ship or crew, he has been imprisoned by the nymph Calypso. Zeus finally sends Hermes to him. The Greek captain builds a ship and sets sail for Ithaca, but Poseidon, still mad at Odysseus for blinding Polyphemus, sends a storm to destroy the hero's ship. With Athena's help, Odysseus lands at Scheria. There he is offered help to return home. First, however, he spends a night telling of all his fantastic adventures since he left Troy.

Odysseus and Calypso in the caves of Ogygia, by Jan Brueghel the Elder (1568–1625)

Ultimately, Odysseus arrives in Ithaca disguised as a beggar. He finds Telemachus, and together they dispatch the suitors. At last Odysseus is reunited with Penelope.

The Odyssey continues to be studied. In 2008, two scientists at Rockefeller University used astronomical clues in the story to determine that April 16, 1178 BCE, was the precise date on which Odysseus arrived home.

The Giant Polyphemus with Galatea and the Herdsman Acis from the Sala Di Amore E Psiche 1528, Giulio Romano, in Italy. Polyphemus tried to woo the water nymph Galatea.

CYCLOPES

CHAPTER 4

The Beast and the Beauty

Considering how foul and nasty Polyphemus acted toward Odysseus, it may be hard to believe he was actually in love once. He was enamoured with a beautiful water nymph named Galatea.

It is uncertain where this story falls in the monster's life. Some say that it happened before Odysseus encountered the Cyclops. Others think it occurred after his visit. If it was indeed after, the story is even more remarkable, because the Cyclops has his eye again.

This story of love comes from the great Roman poet Ovid. It shows a different side of Polyphemus. It is possible that over the years, sympathy began to develop for him, abandoned and blind on his island. As Edith Hamilton says: "This [the Odysseus story] was the only story told about Polyphemus for many years. Centuries passed and he was still the same, a frightful monster, shapeless, huge, his eye put out. But finally he changed, as what is ugly and evil is apt to change and grow milder with time. Perhaps some storyteller saw the helpless, suffering creature Odysseus left behind as a thing to be pitied."[1]

Whenever the story occurred, it is a tale of love, jealousy, and tragedy. Galatea was a beautiful sea nymph, and she stole Polyphemus's heart. The difference between the two could not have been more startling: She was a classic beauty, with pure white skin, soft hair, and ruby lips. He, on the other hand, was an ugly monster. Maybe he was not as hideous as when he had trapped Odysseus and his men in his cave and was eating the hapless Greeks for dinner, but he was ugly just the same. His hair was long, stringy, and full of dust and dirt; his beard was scraggily and knotted; and his pointy teeth were yellow.

To make himself look more presentable to Galatea, the Cyclops used a rake to comb his hair and a scythe to smooth his beard. He even sang a song to the nymph to try to impress her.

None of these things worked, because Galatea was in love with someone else: a sixteen-year-old boy named Acis. The two were quite happy together. As Galatea recalled in Ovid's poem: "I was his only joy, and he was mine."[2]

Try as he might to improve his appearance, Polyphemus could not make Galatea forget the horrible way he had treated guests to his cave, or the men he had eaten. The harder he tried to impress her, the more she fell for Acis. Eventually she did not know which was stronger: her love for Acis or her disdain for Polyphemus. She says, "Ask not which passion in my soul was [higher]. My last aversion, or my first desire."[3]

However, something remarkable happened to Polyphemus as he tried to woo Galatea. His entire temperament changed. He no longer looked to lure unsuspecting sailors into his cave and eat them. Galatea says: "His cruelty, and thirst of blood are lost; And ships securely sail along the coast."[4]

All who knew of the Cyclops's love for Galatea realized that a relationship between the two could never happen. There were too many differences between them. Besides the size difference, Polyphemus was deathly afraid of water. Galatea spent most of her time in the water.

Still, Polyphemus tried. He promised to bring her many gifts, especially of things he found in nature. He tells her:

"I walk'd the mountains, and two cubs I found
(Whose dam [mother] had left 'em on the naked ground),
So like, that no distinction could be seen:
So pretty, they were presents for a queen;
And so they shall; I took them both away;
And keep, to be companions of your play."[5]

Polyphemus Surprising Acis and Galatea, a sculpture at the Medici Fountain in Paris, captures the moment when Polyphemus discovers Galatea is already in love.

However, nothing the Cyclops did could sway Galatea, and finally he began to wonder why she could not love him. He went looking for her, tearing through the woods and the fields of the countryside like a wounded animal.

Meanwhile, Galatea and Acis were frolicking at the water's edge, enjoying each other's company like any two people in love. Suddenly Polyphemus burst out of the woods and came upon them, and in that moment he knew why Galatea had rejected his advances. She was in love with another.

The knowledge that he had a rival enraged the jealous Cyclops. Hurt and angry, he bellowed: "I see, I see; but this shall be your last."[6]

When Galatea heard the Cyclops roar, and saw how mad he was, she quickly dived into the water to escape. Acis was not as quick. Before he could also flee, the angry Cyclops tore off a piece of a mountain and flung it at the youth. The huge piece of rock landed on him, killing him.

In that moment Galatea prayed to the gods that the two could be together forever. As her lover's blood flowed from underneath the giant boulder, it changed into crystal-clear water. Some say that it became the river that flows from the base of Mount Etna in Sicily. Then the giant rock cracked, and from the opening stepped a river god who looked just like Acis. Galatea describes him this way:

"Were not his stature taller than before,
His bulk augmented [increased], and his beauty more,
His colour blue; for Acis he might pass . . . "[7]

This is the tale of Polyphemus and Galatea. There is no further record in Greek myth of the Cyclops ever loving another.

Ovid

Roman poet Ovid is often ranked with Virgil and Homer as one of the most important and influential poets of ancient times. Ovid's proper Latin name was Publius Ovidius Naso. He was born March 20, 43 BCE, in Sulmo, east of Rome. His father wanted him to study law—but Ovid had the heart of a poet, not a lawyer. The death of his brother helped him make a choice. He turned his back on law and began traveling to places such as Athens and Sicily. He had several jobs working for the government, but resigned them all to pursue his writing.

One of Ovid's most celebrated works is *Metamorphoses,* an epic poem he completed about 8 CE. Its characters come from Greek mythology. The overall subject of the poem, as the title suggests, is change—in this case, the human form changes into something in nature. The story of Polyphemus, Galatea, and Acis fits this theme perfectly, since Acis's blood transforms into water upon his death. Other stories in the poem concern other famous human transformations from Greek mythology, such as the tale of Apollo and Daphne, in which the god Apollo pursues Daphne only to have her turn into a tree.

Ovid was banished by Emperor Augustus to Tomis, located on the Black Sea, in 8 CE. He had written about adultery—in Rome, a crime that was punishable by banishment. At Tomis, Ovid tried to continue working, but his writings reflect his loneliness and fondness for Rome. In addition, he certainly missed the companionship of his third wife. He wrote poems dedicated to Augustus in an attempt to gain favor and be recalled to Rome.

Apollo and Daphne, John William Waterhouse, 1908

It was not to be. Ovid died in exile at Tomis in either 17 or 18 CE. There is a statue in the modern Romanian city of Constanta (formerly Tomis) in his honor.

The Cyclops, by Odilon Redon, c. 1914. Redon, a French painter, said that his works are meant to inspire, and are not to be defined.

CYCLOPES

CHAPTER 5

Were Cyclopes Ever Real?

The Cyclopes are obviously mythological characters—but did the Greeks invent them, or did they base them on something from real life?

Some of the possible figures and images that ultimately became the Cyclopes in Greek myth are in the explanation of the one-eyed creatures being master metal smiths and forging great weapons. As Greek myth expert Robert Graves observes, early on there was a group of human smiths who were quite good at working bronze. He describes these bronze smiths as having interlocking rings tattooed on their foreheads, in honor of the sun, which was the source of the fires they used to melt and shape metal. Postulating that *Cyclops* means "ring-eyed," Graves says that smiths used metal rings in their work, as models for things such as bowls and helmets (like using the bottom of a glass to help draw a circle).[1]

Another possible reason that these metalworkers sparked the legends of the Cyclopes is that they used an eye patch. The patch protected one eye from the sparks produced by banging on hot metal. It also gave them the appearance of only having one eye.

Add to this image one final ingredient, and that is the meaning of the names of the first three Cyclopes: Thunder, Lightning, and Brightness.

Now, put everything together: a large man, one eye shaded so that he has just a single eye peering out, with circles tattooed on his forehead, banging on red-hot metal. The noise must have sounded like thunder, the sparks produced like lightning, and the flash of light blindingly bright as the metal-maker hammered his metal. It is easy to see how this image could become the model for the Cyclopes, especially as time passed and the human models were forgotten.[2]

Could this image of one-eyed human beings working with hot metal be the basis for the story of the mythical Cyclopes? Of course no one knows for certain, but it is interesting to speculate.

In 1914 Othenio Abel, an Austrian paleontologist, proposed another theory of the origin of the Cyclops character. Abel theorized that the Cyclops story originated when the ancient Greeks found the skeletons of dwarf elephants.

Scientists speculate that elephants first arrived in the area that includes Sicily about two million years ago. As the years went on, the elephants became smaller, until they were less than a quarter the size of the original woolly mammoths that had first populated the region. These dwarf elephants became extinct about 8,000 years ago, just about the time humans were first migrating into the area. It is extremely likely that the ancient Greeks discovered their skeletons as they began to populate the region.

The skulls of these elephants had an enormous hole where the animal's trunk had been. Consider the reaction of ancient peoples when first coming into contact with these skeletons that had a large hole in the center of the head. Since they had no contact or experience with elephants, isn't it possible that they would have mistaken this hole for a giant eye socket?[3] If they did, it is not too great a leap for the ancients to have imagined that these skeletons once belonged to a race of one-eyed giants that had previously lived on the island.

Ironworkers with a patch over one eye; the skeletons of dwarf elephants—are either of these things the real-life origins of the Cyclops myth? Or was there something else?

According to Greek researcher Robert Garland, Polyphemus is a symbol representing the Greek people's fear of foreign races. Since they had little firsthand knowledge of other peoples, the Greeks had to rely on rumors. As is often the case with rumors, they were wildly

Some theories hold that the idea of the Cyclops may have originated when people found the large trunk hole in the middle of dwarf elephant skulls.

inaccurate. The people they thought lived elsewhere included the Mouthless Ones, who had holes in their faces instead of mouths; the Dogheads, who did not talk but barked; and the Shadowfeet, a race of one-legged people who shaded their body with their one gigantic foot.[4]

The three Cyclopes were originally portrayed as working at the forge. Some theories hold that human forge workers may have inspired the idea of the Cyclopes.

Taken in this context, it is possible that the Cyclops could represent all of their fears of foreign races rolled into one character. As Garland writes: "Solitary, monstrous in size, possessing a single eye in the center of his forehead, stupid, contemptuous toward the gods, hostile toward strangers, ignorant of seafaring and agriculture, Polyphemos [*sic*] is everything that the Greeks despised."[5] He continues: "No figure quite so succinctly epitomizes the horror of the foreign"[6] as the Cyclops.

The three metal-working Cyclopes are not major characters in the Greek myths. Even when discussing their deaths, the tale is as much about Apollo as about the Cyclopes.

An interesting thing to think about is why the Cyclopes were "demoted," so to speak, from helpers and friends of the gods to an evil band of creatures who care nothing for the gods. Polyphemus, the monster who boasted that he cared nothing for Zeus and heartlessly ate Odysseus's men, represents this change. He is a far cry from the three helpful Cyclopes that gave Zeus weapons.

The Cyclops on display at the Natural History Museum in London. This mythological monster remains a popular figure in contemporary culture.

One possibility for the change is that the universe had settled down after all of the chaos of creation, when monsters and gods lived and fought side-by-side. The world became inhabited by gods, who were human-like in appearance, and by humans. Monsters such as the Cyclopes were clearly evil and had no place in a universe populated by humans. In order to banish them from their stories, the people transformed them from good to evil, so that they could be justly defeated by humans and gods.

The character of the Cyclops is still very much a part of modern society. The name Cyclops is still in use today, for various technologies such as computer software and lighting devices.

The Greek city of Mycenae has become a tourist attraction, and is one of the best examples of cyclopean construction—a particular type of construction that uses large, irregular rocks. Cyclopean construction kits are available for people who want to build their own cyclopean-style structures.

In popular culture, the image and name of Cyclops is extremely prevalent. Polyphemus figures prominently in *Percy Jackson and the Olympians: Sea of Monsters*. There is also a Cyclops in the movie *Clash of the Titans*. In the animated television series *Futurama,* the character of spaceship captain Leela is a Cyclops. However, she is extremely intelligent, very kind, and attractive; one of the show's other characters has a crush on her.

The character of Scott Summers in the popular X-Men comic books and movies is named Cyclops because he has to wear a special visor that gives him the appearance of having just one eye. This character is one of the most common ways that people, especially children, are introduced to the word *Cyclops*.

Computer software? Movies? A spaceship captain—and a female? What would Polyphemus think of all this?

Mycenae

The city-state of Mycenae figures prominently in Greek myth. Mycenae was founded by Perseus. He is famous for slaying Medusa, the Gorgon with the snakes in place of hair who could turn men to stone. Perseus married Andromeda but was killed when he went to war against another city, Argos.

Mycenae was then ruled by a man named Atreus. He had two sons, Agamemnon and Menelaus. Agamemnon became the ruler of Mycenae. He married Clytemnestra, and Menelaus married her sister, Helen.

This all ties into the Trojan War, because Helen is the woman that Paris took to Troy. In retaliation for the dishonor shown to his family, Agamemnon launched what became the Trojan War.

In real life, Mycenae was a major Greek city located in southern Greece. It was an extremely strong military city that held much of southern Greece under its thumb. Because of its importance, the period of ancient Greek history from 1600 to 1100 BCE is called the Mycenaean period.

At a date often given as 1350 BCE, the Mycenaean fortifications on the city's acropolis and other hills were rebuilt using massive stones. Because the stones were so large, the building style was called cyclopean—it was thought that only the Cyclopes could have the strength to lift them.

Around 1200 BCE, Mycenae began to decline as a great power. Although it would survive several hundred more years, it would never regain its former importance. By the late Roman years, Mycenae was abandoned.

Excavations at Mycenae began in the nineteenth century. In the early 1870s, Heinrich Schliemann began a complete excavation of the site. One of the most famous structures in Mycenae is the Lion's Gate. It is the main entrance to the fortified citadel.

The Lion's Gate at Mycenae

Chapter 1. Trapped!

1. Edith Hamilton, *Mythology* (New York: New American Library, 1989), p. 82.
2. Ibid.

Chapter 2. The Birth—and Death—of the Cyclopes

1. Jean-Pierre Vernant, *The Universe, the Gods, and Men* (New York: HarperCollins Publishers, 2001), p. 3.
2. Edith Hamilton, *Mythology* (New York: New American Library, 1989), p. 64.
3. Ibid., p. 65
4. Vernant, p. 18.
5. Ibid., p. 21.
6. Ron Leadbetter, Asclepius, *Encyclopedia Mythica,* http://www.pantheon.org/articles/a/asclepius.html

Chapter 3. In the Cave of the Beast

1. Jean-Pierre Vernant, *The Universe, the Gods, and Men* (New York: HarperCollins Publishers, 2001), p. 93.
2. Ibid.
3. Ibid.
4. Ibid., p. 94.
5. Ibid.
6. Edith Hamilton, *Mythology* (New York: New American Library, 1989), p. 84.
7. Ibid.

Chapter 4. The Beast and the Beauty

1. Edith Hamilton, *Mythology* (New York: New American Library, 1989), p. 84.
2. Ovid, Ovid's *Metamorphoses* (New York: The Heritage Press, 1961), p. 446.
3. Ibid.
4. Ibid., p. 447.
5. Ibid., p. 450.

6. Ibid., p. 452.
7. Ibid.

Chapter 5. Were Cyclopes Ever Real?
1. Robert Graves, *The Greek Myths* (London, England: Penguin Books, 1992), p. 32.
2. Ibid.
3. The Classic Pages—*Homer's Odyssey:* "Meet the Original Cyclops," http://www.users.globalnet.co.uk/~loxias/cyclops02.htm.
4. Robert Garland, *Daily Life of the Ancient Greeks* (Westport, Connecticut: Greenwood Press, 1998), p. 77.
5. Ibid.
6. Ibid.

From *Clash of the Titans,* 1981

For Young Adults

Green, Jen. *Myths of Ancient Greece*. Austin, Texas: Raintree Steck-Vaughn, 2001.

Hoena, B.A. *Cyclopes*. Mankato, Minnesota: Capstone Press, 2004.

Houle, Michelle M. *Gods and Goddesses in Greek Mythology*. Berkeley Heights, New Jersey: Enslow Publishers, 2001.

McCarty, Nick. *The Iliad*. Boston, Massachusetts: Kingfisher, 2004.

McGee, Marni. *Ancient Greece: Archeology Unlocks the Secrets of Greece's Past*. Washington, D.C.: National Geographic, 2007.

Tracy, Kathleen. *The Life and Times of Homer*. Hockessin, Delaware: Mitchell Lane Publishers, 2005.

Weber, Belinda. *The Best Book of Ancient Greece*. New York: Kingfisher, 2005.

Works Consulted

Avery, Catherine B., editor. *The New Century Handbook of Greek Mythology and Legend*. New York: Meredith Corporation, 1972.

Burn, Lucilla. *Greek Myths*. Austin, Texas: University of Texas Press, 1990.

Garland, Robert. *Daily Life of the Ancient Greeks*. Westport, Connecticut: Greenwood Press, 1998.

Graves, Robert. *The Greek Myths*. London, England: Penguin Books, 1992.

Guirand, Félix. *Greek Mythology*. London, Great Britain: Batchworth Press Limited, 1963.

Hamilton, Edith. *Mythology*. New York: New American Library, 1989.

Ovid. *Metamorphoses*. New York: The Heritage Press, 1961.

Richardson, Donald. *Great Zeus and All His Children*. Greyden Press, 1993.

Vernant, Jean-Pierre. *The Universe, the Gods, and Men*. New York: HarperCollins Publishers, 2001.

On the Internet

Ancient Greece
  http://ancient-greece.org/

Ancient Greece
  http://www.ancientgreece.com/s/Main_Page

Ancient Greece for Kids
   http://greece.mrdonn.org/
Ancient Greece for Kids
   http://www.historyforkids.org/learn/greeks/

GLOSSARY

chaos (KAY-os)—Total confusion.

contempt (kon-TEMPT)—Scorn.

context (KON-text)—The part of a written or spoken statement that comes before or follows a particular word or phrase and influences its meaning.

decree (deh-KREE)—An order having the force of authority.

discord (DIS-kord)—Dispute.

dispatch (DIS-patch)—To put to death.

epitomize (ee-PIH-toh-myz)—To ideally represent.

grisly (GRIZ-lee)—Horrible.

nymph (NIMF)—One of the beautiful mythological females usually associated with things in nature, such as rivers, trees, and meadows.

paleontologist (pay-lee-on-TOL-uh-jist)—A scientist who studies life-forms from former geologic periods.

paranoia (payr-uh-NOY-uh)—Imagining the total hostility of others.

perilous (PAYR-uh-lis)—Full of risk.

postulate (POS-choo-layt)—To make a claim.

prevalent (PREH-vuh-lunt)—Widespread.

scythe (SYTH)—A tool with a long, curved blade used for cutting grass or grains by hand.

succinct (suk-SINKT)—Expressed in a few words.

INDEX

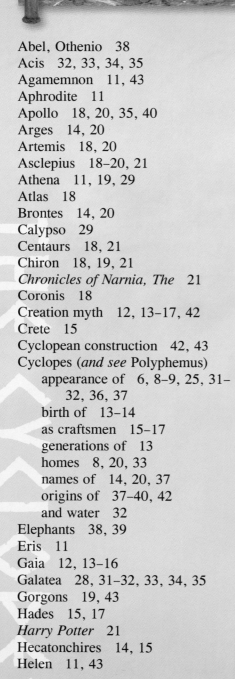